LITERATURE

LITERATURE
A Student's Guide to Research and Writing

Robert Skapura
and
John Marlowe

Libraries Unlimited, Inc.
Englewood, Colorado
1988

Copyright © 1988 Robert Skapura and John Marlowe
All Rights Reserved
Printed in the United States of America

No part of this publication may be reproduced, stored in a retrieval system, or transmitted, in any form or by any means, electronic, mechanical, photocopying, recording, or otherwise, without the prior written permission of the publisher.

LIBRARIES UNLIMITED, INC.
P.O. Box 3988
Englewood, Colorado 80155-3988

Library of Congress Cataloging-in-Publication Data

Skapura, Robert.
   Literature : a student's guide to research and writing / Robert Skapura and John Marlowe.
   v, 46 p. 17x25 cm.
   ISBN 0-87287-650-0
   1. English language--Rhetoric. 2. Criticism--Authorship.
3. Report writing. I. Marlowe, John, 1938-   II. Title.
PE1479.C7S53   1988
808'.042--dc19   88-8513
                                                                                     CIP

Contents

I   CHOOSING A TOPIC 1

II   BEGINNING RESEARCH 8

III   TAKING NOTES 16

IV   ORGANIZING 25

V   WRITING 29

VI   REPORT AND TERM PAPER FORMAT 33

I
Choosing a Topic

1. You will write reports or papers for three reasons.

All through your formal education you will write reports. Teachers and schools very often require them. You may even write reports in some future job. Whatever the extent of your writing, the papers you prepare will require three things of you:

1. To prove that you can gather information from many sources

2. To prove that you know something about a particular subject

3. To present a theory, a plan of action, a proposal, a statement, or a conclusion, which you will support with logic, persuasion, and facts.

2. Reports focus on a single subject and a conclusion.

Most school reports concern a single subject with few if any subtopics. They call for information, summaries, facts, and then, most important, *conclusions*. You must *say* something, not just repeat what you've read. For reports the sources are usually fewer. Footnotes and a bibliography are usually not required.

3. A report is not a term paper.

A report is less complex than a term paper. Term papers have larger topics, demanding more extensive research and information from a large number of sources. The way you write and the form you use are more important for a term paper than for a report. A report is shorter, frequently less than ten pages in length.

CHOOSING A TOPIC

It is important to know which you are expected to write. It is crucial that you and your teacher agree on what you are expected to do. If you turn in a report when you are expected to write a term paper, you will receive a bad grade. If you write a term paper when a report is all that is required, you will have wasted a lot of energy. Your teacher may use different words for what you are required to write, so be sure that you understand exactly what is expected of you. Most teachers will give you a clear, concise description of how you should present your ideas.

A report focuses on a single aspect of a topic. A term paper is, in a sense, made up of many short reports. The thought process and the development of a conclusion are common to both reports and term papers.

4. In literature classes, there are two kinds of papers.

Literature papers are of two types: analytical and research. An analytical paper, as the word implies, asks you to develop ideas about the meaning of a particular work or body of works. What you write grows out of your personal analysis of the work itself (the novel, the play, the poem, etc.).

A research paper asks you first to gather information about a particular work, an author, or even things outside the work itself that will help you better understand literature. *This manual deals only with research papers.*

5. A research paper presents your ideas.

In research papers (whether reports or term papers), *you* present ideas. This is one of the major skills learned in school. Teaching you how to do this is one of the responsibilities of your teachers. Learning how to do this is one of your responsibilities.

6. Use information, don't just repeat it.

To present ideas, you must paraphrase and line up various bits of repeatable and respectable information—not claiming it as your own, rather, demonstrating that you understand it and can make use of it. Your teachers want you to learn more about an area of your studies and to understand it well enough to make an original point about it (an original point for you, original for this class at this school at this time, not a point that is fresh for all of Western civilization).

7. **If possible, choose a topic that is attractive to you.**

To start, your teacher will give you a couple of words, a few choices, perhaps a list of authors, time periods, a literary movement, topics related to your class work—all in all, a variety of subjects, one of which you must write about intelligently. After going over the possibilities, choose a topic that is appealing to you for some reason. If you can choose one that is genuinely pleasing and interesting, you are way ahead. If you cannot, you will have to pretend, and you will have to pretend so well that you will convince yourself and your teacher that you genuinely care about your choice.

Because the purpose of most literature is to reflect our society and recreate the human experience, you have a unique opportunity to choose subject matter that is directly related to your experience, values, and concerns.

Most librarians can suggest topics not only because they know what resources are readily available for research, but because they are familiar with what other students have already done successfully. Ask the librarian before you begin.

8. **Never use the length of a literary work as the reason for choosing a topic.**

Some students choose a topic because the works or the books related to the topic are short, figuring a topic with thin books is easier than a topic with thick books. Students who choose topics with short books do so because they have not had the experience of reading a book that stirs them to think about ideas that are important to them.

An author chooses the length of work to fit the purpose of his or her point. That point may be simple or complex. The social implications of a work are not connected to the number of words in a work. Herman Melville's *Billy Budd* is shorter than Ken Kesey's *One Flew Over the Cuckoo's Nest*. Both books are rich in topics for research, but the modern reader would most likely enjoy a topic related to the longer book. Again, your teacher or librarian can be a great source of information about the appropriate book for your skills and assignment.

9. **No topic is easy, but some are less difficult than others.**

As a rule literary research papers help the researcher gain historical background, literary background, or knowledge of an author's life or work. No topic is easy, but some *are* less difficult. No matter what your subject, if information is plentiful and easy to find, the writing will be

4 / CHOOSING A TOPIC

easier. Subjects for which there is little information will make the subsequent steps of writing your paper all the more difficult.

10. It is easier to write about older books and authors from the past.

More information has been written about significant writers and literature of three hundred years ago than about something written three months ago. References, descriptions, biographies, and commentaries can be found in reference books, texts, and periodicals. As a rule there's more material about older literature and it is more accessible. The literary events of the last few years are recorded only in newspapers and magazines, and few, if any, books. Contemporary literature may be easier to read, but it is not always easier to research or write about.

11. Specific topics are easier to research than general ones.

It is easier to gather information for specific topics than it is for broad, general ones. General subjects contain too much information. Furthermore, general subjects are not always in the indexes of books. A narrow topic is easier to handle. Look at the following examples:

General	*Specific*
Blacklisting and Anti-Communism	McCarthyism and Dalton Trumbo
The Beat Generation	On the road with Jack Kerouac
Paris in the twenties	Gertrude Stein's literary and artistic circle
Greek Drama	The role of the chorus in Greek Drama
Literature in the Dark Ages	The tragic love of Abelard and Heloise

12. Serious literature frequently demands a background that young people do not yet have.

Serious literature frequently expects the reader to know things beyond the work itself. A popular novel can be enjoyed by anyone who can read. In a sense, the work expects nothing more than that the reader sit back and enjoy it. And that's how popular works should be. It is not much different from going to a popular movie or a concert. More serious works, especially those considered "classics" or those that were influential in their time, require that the reader bring a certain understanding to the reading of the work. This is why books considered classics are read in a classroom setting, where a teacher can provide the background as the work is discussed. One of the goals of a research paper in literature is to teach you how to acquire that background on your own. The subject of such research usually falls into one of four areas.

13. Research topics in literature usually fall into four main categories.

First, there is a paper on a particular **work**, a play, a novel, a poem, that deserves examination as part of our literary heritage. Second, there are papers on an **author** or group of authors. Third, there are **literary movements**. Literature both reflects and helps shape the changes in society. One author influences another and we find that looking back on a period of time, we can see a pattern or style that became popular or widespread. Classicism gave way to Romanticism. which was followed by Realism. We can see similar changes in our own lifetime in music, art, and filmmaking. Lastly, every field has its own set of **concepts or ideas** that help explain and give insight to a work. For example, an understanding of the characteristics of satire, tragic hero, symbolism, and the anti-hero is sometimes necessary to understanding a work.

14. Some works require historical background to understand them.

Whether your topic is a specific work, an author, a literary movement, or a literary concept, it may require historical background. Some works, especially those that were written long ago, are difficult to understand or are very confusing because the customs, beliefs, or social setting are so different from modern times that the story, the characters, their motives, or actions seem incomprehensible. The work itself requires that you know the historical circumstances in which the story is set or when the author was writing.

It would be difficult to understand *The Scarlet Letter* without some knowledge of Puritan society. Likewise, knowing how factory workers were treated in the early 1900s gives added insight to *The Jungle*. The play *The Crucible* by Arthur Miller is about the Salem witchcraft trials, but if you understand that the author was writing during the McCarthy hearings of the 1950s, in which people were hunting for Communists in the United States, the play takes on another dimension.

Historical background here does not always mean knowing significant political or military events. Rather, it is the *social history* that is important: what ordinary people thought, what people believed in, what was happening in society.

15. Some works require literary background.

Some books require that the reader understand the literary conventions of the time. For example, reading a classic Greek play requires that you know how the Greek theater was physically structured, the role the chorus played, and how the actors were dressed and costumed. We are so used to "realistic" plays and films that a Greek play, viewed without an understanding of the literary conventions of the times, appears stiff and stilted.

Likewise, understanding literary terms such as tragic hero, romanticism, and realism gives the reader insight into works that were written in those traditions. For example, in everyday speech "tragic" usually means very sad or disastrous. But the term *tragedy* and the role of the "tragic hero" have very special meanings in literature that have little to do with the emotion of sadness. A paper that centers on a literary convention usually defines and describes the terms and then applies them to a particular work. For example, after a lengthy description of the characteristics of a tragic hero, one could look at Hamlet to see whether he fits that role.

Another kind of literary background is the knowledge of well-known stories that are used or alluded to in later works. For example, the legend of King Arthur, the story of Cain killing Abel, and the doomed love of Romeo and Juliet have a way of working themselves into later works with a slightly different twist.

16. Knowledge of an author's life frequently gives insight to the work.

Most authors write about things taken directly or indirectly from their own lives; thus, knowing more about the author's life very often helps one to understand the author's work and his or her intentions when he wrote it. This is not to say that all works are autobiographical, only that it is impossible *not* to be influenced by events in one's life. When reading about an author, you should look for those powerful events that helped shaped him or her as a person. You should also try to understand what things the author felt strongly about and then look for the expression of those beliefs in the literary work.

17. A research paper in literature has three parts.

As you search, keep reminding yourself that a good paper about literature has three major ingredients:

1. Background information about the author or the work

2. The ideas of other writers

3. Your ideas

Or, put another way, begin with good information; find someone else's; develop your own based on the first two. Usually you develop your ideas after you find someone else's.

Most often you will find other writers' ideas in the library. The material there tells you about time periods in which you have never lived, history you did not witness, and interesting people you never met. The sources are amazingly rich, and it is to your eternal advantage to know how to unlock this single most important warehouse of knowledge.

II
Beginning Research

18. Begin your research in the library.

You enter the library with a general idea of your topic. You do not have a good solid defendable idea yet, but you will. At this point, you are sparring with your topic. You are ready to begin your research. The first thing you need is more information, more than the few words contained in your topic. You have to gather it. You probably don't know anyone who lived with William Faulkner or worked in China with Pearl Buck or hitch-hiked with Jack Kerouac. You don't have the experience in literature or psychology to theorize about the creation of Sylvia Plath's poetry, so you will have to go to other sources to get your information.

19. Start your research in reference books, not the card catalog.

Unless you know a great deal about your subject already, begin your research in reference works. If you go directly to the card catalog, you are hoping to find an entire book (or more) about your topic. Often there are no whole books on your subject. That doesn't mean that there's no information. There might be a great many books each with a chapter or two on your topic, but if there's not an *entire* book all on your topic, it won't be listed in the card catalog. So, instead, begin your research in the reference section of the library. Reference books will give you a short summary, usually a page or less, on your topic. The most basic reference work is, of course, an encyclopedia. But in every subject area there are also special books. These large and expensive books are often found in a special reference section of the library and very often they cannot be checked out. The fact that they cannot be checked out should not matter, because you will be reading just a short section from each.

20. Choose the best reference book from the list provided or ask the librarian.

A scholar in a particular field will know the best reference books in that subject area. As a student you can't be expected to know those titles. At the end of this chapter is a list of some of the most helpful reference books that deal with literature. Your library may contain more recent or even better reference books than we've listed. If none of the ones we've listed covers your topic, ask the librarian for a suggestion.

21. Get a general notion about your subject from reference books.

To begin your research, you must get an overview, a general picture of your topic. In literature, this means knowing these four things:

1. the author(s) involved in your topic

2. the time period in which your author wrote

3. the time period in which the work is set

4. the nationality of the author

Books that contain information about authors and their works are frequently divided by nationality, time period, and the kind of works the author wrote (novels, plays, poetry, etc.). (For example, in *Contemporary Novelists* you will find information about Ken Kesey because he is a modern American novelist, but the same book will not have anything about Voltaire, an eighteenth century French poet and dramatist.) If you don't know even this much about your topic or author, you should begin in some general reference books:

Benét's Reader's Encyclopedia

Encyclopedia Americana

Encyclopaedia Britannica

Remember, when using general reference books, you'll be looking for the author(s), the time period, and the nationality of the author or the country in which the work is set. Knowing these things will allow you to use the more extensive reference books listed at the end of this chapter.

Occasionally a contemporary writer sets his or her work in a distant time period. Mary Renault sets most of her novels in ancient Greece, so it

10 / BEGINNING RESEARCH

is important to understand the *time period* about which she is writing; you will still have to know when the author lived, however, to find information about *her* as a writer.

22. If little or nothing is found in reference books, one of three things is true.

If after you have tried a number of reference works you have found little or nothing, one of three things has happened:

1. Your subject is so recent that little or nothing has been written about it in book form. This means that you will have to go to a magazine index. The most common magazine index is the *Readers' Guide to Periodical Literature.*

2. Your subject is so obscure that only special books on that subject, instead of broad reference works, will contain the information you need. You may have to go to a larger library, get additional help from your teacher or librarian, or consider choosing another topic.

3. The word or words you have chosen to look up are not the words used by the authors of reference works to describe that topic. Ask the librarian for alternatives to the words you have been using.

In the yellow pages of the telephone directory nothing will be found under *Doctors* or *Cars*. The "right" words are *Physicians* and *Automobiles*. There's no way to know this except from experience. Likewise books and libraries use some words and do not use others. Your teacher or librarian can help you figure out what words would be most promising if you suspect that the topic you've chosen might be found under a different heading.

23. Only after getting a notion about your subject should you go to the card catalog.

If you are fortunate, the card catalog will lead you to one or more books about your topic. But even if the card catalog produces nothing *directly*, if you have gotten a notion of your subject from reference books you can continue to search the card catalog *indirectly*. An example will make this clear:

Topic: The plight of the Okies in *The Grapes of Wrath*: exaggeration or reality?

Going to *Benét's Reader's Encyclopedia* you will find information by looking under both *Grapes of Wrath* and Steinbeck, John:

People: John Steinbeck, novelist

Time period of the author: 1902-1968

Nationality: American

Time period of the work: 1930s

If going to the card catalog now produces little or nothing on *The Grapes of Wrath* except the novel itself, you can continue your search for information indirectly. The two most helpful areas to search will be information about the author's life and information about the time period in which the work is set. Whole biographies exist on John Steinbeck, and there are history books which describe the 1930s.

24. Look especially for books about the author.

Books about the author are so helpful that they deserve to be sought out. Once you have established the nationality and the time period of your author, you should have no trouble finding information in reference books.

You must remember one thing, however, when looking for books about authors in the card catalog. Books by an author and books about an author will both have the author's name at the top of the catalog card, last name first, followed by a comma, and then the first name. Books *about* the author have the author's name in *all upper case letters*. Books *by* an author are in *both upper and lower case letters*.

Examples:

Books about an author: author is upper case.

```
         STEINBECK, JOHN
810.9    Ferrell, Keith
Fer         John Steinbeck: The voice of the land,
         by Keith Ferrell.  M. Evans, c1986
            191 p.  index
```

Books by an author: author is upper and lower case.

```
917.3    Steinbeck, John
Ste         Travels with Charley; in search of
         America.  Viking, c1962
            246p.
```

25. Books about literary history are very different from general history books.

There is a special kind of history book that will be helpful for topics in literature. These are books of literary history. They concern themselves with what was happening socially, that is, what events, movements, and trends influenced the authors who were writing in that time period. They often describe how one author influenced another and how writing styles reflect the period in which they were written.

In the card catalog these books will be found by looking for the literature of a certain nationality followed by the words HISTORY AND CRITICISM.

Examples: AMERICAN LITERATURE – HISTORY AND
CRITICISM
RUSSIAN LITERATURE – HISTORY AND
CRITICISM

or just

LITERATURE – HISTORY AND CRITICISM

26. Look also for historical books about the time period.

"Time period" here could mean the setting of the literary work, the time period in which the author was writing, or both. Once you've established the time period of your subject from reference books, you should have no trouble finding books that cover that era. Historians frequently write about just a certain period of time, for example, the 1920s, the Depression, or the 1960s.

You must remember one thing when looking for "time period" books in the card catalog. The card catalog groups books about a particular time period *by country* first, followed by the word HISTORY.

Examples: AFRICA – HISTORY
ENGLAND – HISTORY
UNITED STATES – HISTORY
UNITED STATES – HISTORY – COLONIAL
PERIOD
UNITED STATES – HISTORY – CIVIL WAR
UNITED STATES – HISTORY – 1961-1974

27. Summary.

1. Get an overview of your topic from reference books.

    Author and the *Kind of works written*

    Time period in which the author wrote

    Nationality of the author

    Time period in which the work is set

2. Look for books *directly* about your topic in the card catalog.

3. Look for books *indirectly* about your topic in the card catalog (that is, about the author or the time period of either the author or the work, depending on which is more relevant).

Helpful Books for Getting an Overview of the Topic

General Reference

Encyclopaedia Britannica. 30 vols. Chicago: Encyclopaedia Britannica.

Encyclopedia Americana. 30 vols. New York: Grolier.

General Literature Reference

Benét's Reader's Encyclopedia. New York: Harper and Row.

The Oxford Companion to American Literature. New York: Oxford Univ. Press.

The Oxford Companion to English Literature. New York: Oxford Univ. Press.

The Oxford Companion to French Literature. New York: Oxford Univ. Press.

Authors — General

Cyclopedia of World Authors. 3 vols. Englewood Cliffs, N.J.: Salem Press.

McGraw-Hill Encyclopedia of World Biography. 12 vols. New York: McGraw-Hill.

Authors — Before 1900

American Authors 1600-1900. New York: H. W. Wilson.

British Authors of the 19th Century. New York: H. W. Wilson.

British Authors before 1800. New York: H. W. Wilson.

European Authors 1000-1900. New York: H. W. Wilson.

Authors — Twentieth Century

Twentieth Century Authors. New York: H. W. Wilson.

World Authors 1950-1970. New York: H. W. Wilson.

World Authors 1970-1975. New York: H. W. Wilson.

World Authors 1975-1980. New York: H. W. Wilson.

Authors — Contemporary

Contemporary Authors. 114 vols. Detroit: Gale Research Co.

Contemporary Novelists. New York: St. Martin's Press.

Contemporary Dramatists. New York: St. Martin's Press.

Contemporary Poets. New York: St. Martin's Press.

III
Taking Notes

The third step in report writing is by far the most difficult. It is also the most important. If you skip this step you will stay up very late the last few nights before your paper is due, and most probably you will copy whole sections out of a few of the books and magazines you've collected, putting these sections together with only a few words of your own. You'll learn little, write a stilted paper, and bore both your teachers and yourself.

You will also more than likely plagiarize. Plagiarism is repeating someone else's words as if they are your own. This is such a serious offense that there are laws against it. Too often students do this because they are anxious to *present* information instead of *using* it. Remember, you are gathering information the same way you gather tools and material to make something. You are gathering information to put it to use. Your final product will be your words, not somebody else's.

28. As you read take notes on things of importance.

This advice is both obvious and useless at the same time. Of course you should take notes on important things. But it begs the question, How can you *tell* when you've read something important?

In literature classes you look at:

- the literary work itself

- significant events in the author's life

- significant historical events in the time of the author's life

- significant events in the time period of the work

- significant literary movements and trends
- literary techniques of the writer

Your report topic will probably be in one of these areas. Therefore, as you look for appropriate research material in literature, you should take notes on the following:

Events that
- were important in the writer's life
- may have influenced the work

Dates
- important in the writer's life
- of historical importance to the work

Connections between
- the writer's personal life and his literary work
- literary movements before, during, and after the writer's time
- your writer and another writer
- your writer's work and another work

Descriptions of
- people who influenced your writer
- places that influenced your writer

Explanations of
- literary terms, concepts, or movements
- the personal philosophy of your writer
- how historical setting adds insight to the work
- how things were done, especially if it's dramatically different from today

Examples that
- illustrate your major points
- entertain and illuminate

29. A note is first an idea.

Unless you are actually quoting from a book, your notes should be a summary of what you've read. This sounds like more work than is necessary, when it is so easy to copy whole pages on copy machines that are conveniently found in almost every library. But summarizing *now* makes writing *later* much easier. Copying, by hand or by machine, provides you only with material, not ideas. To summarize requires that you think about the subject; to copy requires only hand-eye coordination or money for the copy machines. Summarizing twenty, thirty, or fifty useful bits of information (descriptions, explanations, powerful examples) will give you the basis to pose the single question that will help you form the thesis of your paper. The important point of this part of the writing is to get you to think about the subject. That is of the utmost importance.

30. Each note must be put on a different slip of paper or card.

This may sound trivial, but it is not. There are many systems for gathering your information. If you continue writing after your formal schooling, you'll probably develop your own. You may already have a computer with a word processor, but before you start typing into your machine, you need to have a system merely to bring good information *to* the computer. Right now, while you're still trying to figure out what you are going to say and how you're going to say it, take a system that has worked for many people for many years.

A note may be a few words or a number of sentences; in either case it should be about one specific subject. A note may take the form of an outline, a question, a summary, or a quotation. We'll describe all four later.

Get a stack of cards. Many people use 3-by-5-inch index cards, but these are frequently too small; 5-by-8-inch cards might be better. Use whatever you're comfortable with, perhaps even slips of paper. Put each note on a separate note card, even if there's room for more. If the note is too long to fit on one card, either write on the back of the card or continue on another card, which should then be stapled to the first one so they are treated as one note. This will become very important later. Each note card will contain two things: the note and the citation. The citation simply tells you where you found that information. The first time you note anything from a particular book or magazine, you should write all the bibliographic information for that source. This is usually the author, title, place of publication, publisher, copyright date, and the page number(s).

Example: Horan, James D. *The Desperate Years*. New York: Crown, 1962. p. 163.

This will make it easy to relocate the book if you need additional information. Also, this makes writing the bibliography easy. Since the bibliography is, unfortunately, usually the last thing done, it is often typed late at night the day before it is due, well after the library is closed. If it is not already on a card, it is sometimes impossible to locate this information at the last minute.

Once you have copied the full citation on the first card, you need not continue to include all the information about that book on your other cards. The title, or an abbreviation of it, followed by the page number(s) should suffice for any other notes taken from the same book.

Example: *Desperate Years*, 163

or

DY 163

There is no set form that notes must follow. You will immediately develop your own style, and as you write more, you will modify it; but once again, let us show you four styles that have worked well for a lot of writers.

To illustrate the various forms notes take, the following selection from *The Desperate Years** has been included as an example of historical background. This excerpt is a quick overview of the Dust Bowl. The subject of this report might be called "The reality of *The Grapes of Wrath*."

> The grass was dead. In the Dakotas, Nebraska, Kansas, Oklahoma, and Texas, the winds were blowing away the topsoil, millions and millions of tons. All that was left was the ugly barren clay. On the morning of November 11, 1933, the first great black cloud rose over America's Dust Bowl, darkening the sky as far east as Albany. It was the first of the blizzards that swept the Great Plains in 1933, 1934, and 1935, laying waste millions of farm and grazing acres.
>
> In 1934, after a year's futile fight against the desolation and the black winds, refugees from America's Sahara began

---

*James D. Horan, *The Desperate Years* (New York: Crown Publishers, Inc., 1962), 163. Reprinted with permission.

moving westward in ancient jalopies. So many left Oklahoma that the name Okie was applied to all the migrants. They jammed U.S. Highway 30 through the Idaho hills, 66 across New Mexico and Arizona, or the old Spanish Trail through El Paso and then westward. The cars and trucks were piled high with torn mattresses, cooking utensils, chamber pots, and bedsprings. Grimy children peered out from behind the junk and gaunt, sad-eyed women looked out of the broken windows of the truck cabs and front seats of the old cars.

It was a vast, confused migration. Side by side with the Okies were fruit tramps from Oregon and cotton pickers from Alabama. When they reached the golden land of California, they fought each other for jobs. The market became glutted and jobs became so scarce that Hoovervilles—now an established part of the big city scene—sprang up all over California.

The permanent citizens became wary of the ragged, disheveled men and women and their dirty-faced children. "Get 'em going" they told the sheriffs, and the deputies with clubs drove the strangers out past the community's limits. The man from southeastern Colorado had suddenly become a "red," a "commie," a bomb-thrower of the worst sort. He was never considered a fellow citizen down in his luck, a man with his family who had had to flee from an avenging nature.

Human error and greed were behind the whole tragedy. In the beginning the Great Plains had been a sea of grass, first for the buffalo, then for the cattle barons. Before the end of the century the range had been badly damaged by overgrazing. Then came the sod busters, the homesteaders who tried to cultivate their 160-acre plots....

There never had been much rain. The annual rainfall was only 10 to 20 inches on the plains as compared with around 40 in the Mississippi Valley region. The years 1930 to 1933 brought drought to the plains....

Government census figures for 1934 and 1935 showed the displaced farmers went to the towns. But there too they met resentment; relief rolls doubled and competition for jobs was fierce. The black blizzards moved across the sky until 1936, when the first green shoots began to appear in the black wilderness. By that time rotation farming was becoming accepted, soil-protective measures were instituted, and men were returning to dig their rusted machinery out of drifts higher than a man.

31. Notes may be in formal or informal outline style:

  I Weather had great impact.
     A. Blizzards blew away top soil   ('33-'35)
     B. Drought made things worse   ('30-'33)

 II "Man" created problems
     A. Greed
     B. Bad farming techniques

III Farmers found it impossible to farm
     A. No top soil
     B. No water

 IV Farmers headed West for jobs and better farms

  V Travel was rough
     A. "Okies"
     B. Terrible conditions on the road
     C. Hoovervilles

 VI Hope returned to the land   ('36)
     A. Grass began to grow
     B. Laws protected soil
     C. Rotation farming

This seems to be exactly the same pattern as the book.

Desperate Years, p. 163

Notice that we have made a note about the pattern of events in the book (*The Grapes of Wrath*) and in the historical time (as shown by *The Desperate Years*). This is the important step that we have been writing about: making the information yours.

32. Notes may be questions and personal responses to yourself:

People were called Okies. What's that like today?

What were Hoovervilles? What about homeless?

Sounds like Steinbeck was not only accurate then, but maybe even now.

What parts of G of W match the info in this article?

DY, 163

33. Notes can be crucial facts:

"... the winds were blowing the top soil, millions and millions of tons ..."

"... laying to waste millions of farm and grazing acres ..."

"In the beginning the Great Plains had been a sea of grass ..."

Homesteaders tried to cultivate 160 acres.

annual rain fall was 10-20 inches

All of this makes me think it was a human problem and a natural one at the same time. Check back with novel.

Source: DY 163-65

34. Notes can be quotes:

"The black blizzards moved across the sky until 1936, when the first green shoots began to appear in the black wilderness. By that time rotation farming was becoming accepted, soil-protective measures were instituted, and men were returning to dig their rusted machinery out of drifts higher than a man."
In GW, the Joads never did get a chance to go back.

Source: DY-165

---

35. Notes can be summaries:

The weather created many problems for the farmers, and these seemed to be connected with other problems created by abuses of the land. The "Okies" could not deal with the problems of the land, and they had to find new places to farm, so they took off for California and the West. But when they got to the west, they found out that things were not as they expected. All of this seems to be pretty much like the information in the book. "Human error and greed were behind the whole tragedy." That quote seems to really tie in with Steinbeck.

D Years/165

36. Notes can be a simple listing of chronological items:

```
Nov. 11 '33 1st blizzard

'33-'35 blizzards continued

'34 Beginning of movement to the West

'30-'34 Drought (?---Does a blizzard have rain?  Why a drought when
there's a lot of blizzards?

'34-'35 Farmers started moving into towns.

'36 some signs of relief.

How does all of this compare to book?

Desperate-163
```

37. Keep a good supply of cards in the books you are reading.

As you read books away from the library or your study, you will often want to take notes. If you have ten or so cards to stick in every book you read, you will be able to take notes at any time, and you will not have to try to remember difficult material or write in a book.

It is quite permissible to write in your own books. Students do it all the time. Remember, though, that although writing notes in a book is often a sign of a serious reader, writing in a book that belongs to someone else is wrong: it is selfish and inconsiderate. Furthermore, if you make it a practice to keep cards in your books, you will be able to write your paper later from a handful of notes rather than from an armload of books.

38. The form your notes take will be just a matter of style, your style.

There is no right or wrong way to make note cards as long as the essential information and the sources are recorded. Good notes and lots of them will make the writing of your paper much easier. We cannot encourage you enough to write notes that require thinking and that start your writing. Although there is no "correct" number of notes to take, beginning writers should have *at least* thirty. They really need more, and good writers always have more. As we say in many places, the more information you have, the better your work will be.

IV
Organizing

By now you have gathered most if not all of your information, and you have to get it into some kind of manageable form, some way to present it in an organized, understandable way that will make the point you wish to make. You have all of the ingredients that you will need, but you have to give them form so they make sense. At this point some students want to start writing, figuring that it is best to get the thing over and done with. While this is an understandable way to feel, the danger of writing a poorly organized, disjointed paper is too great. Most likely your teacher will require that you present your information according to some pattern. What you need first is a pattern for your notes.

39. Reread your note cards and put a key word or words at the top.

This is a crucial step. It is important that you have some sense of each card. You will organize your information at the next step, so you should have some idea what each card covers. What is its major point? Do you begin to see your information take shape? Do you begin to see it leading you to some conclusion? If you have involved yourself with the information already, using it, thinking about it, working with it as you go along, this should be easy.

For example, look at our card in number 33 in the last chapter. When we reread it, we would write "Weather" at the top.

40. Put the cards into piles of related information.

You should have information that begins to follow a pattern or sequence. The best, the most exciting, kind of information is that which lines itself up according to ideas.

Continuing our example, we might begin to accumulate cards in the category of "Problems Created by Nature." Another might be "Conditions of Poverty." Still others might be "California," "Economics," or "Hope." Put them together in stacks. Usually you will have about four groupings, with some left over that you do not know what to do with.

41. You might have some cards that do not fit anywhere. Put those aside.

You may use this information later. You might find that it fits somewhere else, or you might find that you do not need it at all. You also might find that you want to add it at some place just to make your writing better.

There is no such thing as too much information. You can *present* too much information, making your paper boring, but you cannot *have* too much to draw from.

42. Write a sentence or two that describes the contents of each stack.

This is the first step in organizing your ideas on paper. You begin to build your essay. You want to get a clear indication of what you want to write, where you want to go with this report.

Keeping with our example, you might find a lot of information about economic factors beyond the control of people like the Joad family, the main characters in the novel *The Grapes of Wrath*. You would write a sentence about that stack that says, "According to Steinbeck and according to the reference works, economic forces beyond their control affected people like the Joads."

Another stack might have descriptions of living conditions for families and your sentence would be, "It seems like the 'Okies' had severe living conditions because of their poverty."

Do that with each stack of cards, so you have a sentence for each stack. Write down these sentences on a separate sheet of paper.

This is the beginning of your outline.

43. Go back through your cards now to see if you want to change any around.

For example, some of the things that you identified as economic factors might go into a section about weather. Also, some notes in the unused pile might fit now.

44. The final step before starting to write is to pose the single question that your paper will answer.

By this time you should be getting an overall idea of what your paper is going to say. To get this into a single statement, organize the statements around a single question. Your sentences for each stack might be something like this:

1. According to Steinbeck and the reference works, economic forces controlled the Joads and people like them.

2. It seems "The Okies" in the book and in the reference works had severe living conditions.

3. Weather creates serious problems.

4. Traveling from the South to the West was difficult.

5. There seems to be hope at the end of the novel and in the research.

Now, read these carefully and think of a question that covers all of them. In our example, we come up with "Does the novel realistically portray what happened to many of the farmers in the 1930s?"

45. Answer your question with a single sentence. This will be your thesis sentence, the controlling idea of your report.

The thesis statement controls your paper. It is the umbrella under which all of your report fits. It is the sum of your report, the idea you wish to pass on. This is the absolute key to everything.

Think back and you will see that you have gathered a great deal of information, and you channeled it to make a clear idea that you will present to someone else. This is a great skill.

Taking our question from number 44, we would write our thesis sentence as follows: "The historical facts and social events of the 1930s are accurately reflected in John Steinbeck's novel *The Grapes of Wrath*."

46. The more specific or concrete your thesis statement is, the easier the writing will be.

Writing a paper about the connection between a novel and the historical events in it is much easier than writing one about "Depression Novels." Students get in trouble when they have not thought enough

28 / ORGANIZING

about their ideas and when their subject is too general and too hard to write about. The more specific or concrete you get, the easier your writing task will be, especially if you have gathered a lot of good information and you have thought about it.

47. Write an outline.

Your teacher will probably require some kind of outline, but if he or she doesn't, write one anyway. It is important for writing of any kind. Even if it is a couple of notes jotted down, it will do you good. Very, very few writers can get away with starting with the first word and ending with the last without an outline.

Go back to the cards, using our examples, and you will find that our model report can be blocked out in the simplest way as follows:

Thesis statement: The historical facts and social events of the 1930s are accurately reflected in John Steinbeck's novel *The Grapes of Wrath*.

1. Economic factors: From *G of W* and history books.

2. Living conditions: novel, and other books.

3. Weather: Be sure to use description of dust bowl. Mention winds.

4. Difficulty of travel.

5. Hope: Rose O'Sharon and quote from *DY* about digging out rusted machinery.

As you can see this kind of paper might be interesting to write, because it would give you a chance to write about an important topic in a way that would involve you and the reader. It would be interesting and challenging to compare a novel with its historical antecedents in a way that helps you appreciate and understand literature and use the information you are trying to learn. You will, through the outline and through thinking about the material as you gather evidence, learn how to organize and use information.

Some writers will find a more formal outline helpful, and some teachers will require it. Other people will be able to rough out their ideas in an even simpler format than we show here. Our advice is that the more information you gather, the better and easier it is to write. Outlining is just one more way to think about and use the information.

V
Writing

You now have a thesis statement, an outline, and your notes. You know basically what you are going to write; now all you have to do is write it. This is not as hard as it sounds. Your basic structure is already built and your back-up information is ready.

48. Begin in the middle.

Your natural inclination will be to write the paper at once, from beginning to end, from the first word to the last. This is just what you do *not* want to do.

Instead, go through your notes and expand them into longer sentences and paragraphs, roughly following your outline. Connect the cards when you can. Take the most important ones and write expanded versions of them, weaving them into support for an idea. Usually, you should take the sentence that you used to describe the stack, and start writing from that. Or you may want to just string your notes into a couple of sentences, see what you have, then expand those sentences into paragraphs. As a rough rule of thumb, you will want a paragraph for each stack, but that is a simple minimum. You will have thought well about this assignment by now and you can probably write more than that.

Write roughly and freely about each of the points on your cards. This kind of writing should be done with a lot of room on the paper. Skip a lot of spaces; write on every other line; use a lot of paper.

49. Go back through what you have written roughly and mark what you like. Make notes to yourself where you should expand, improve, or cut.

You should have a very, very rough version of the report you are going to write, at least one paragraph for each controlling sentence. Your paper is now beginning to take a rough shape. You are sketching in the shape, choosing the words and the patterns of the ideas.

50. Go back over your outline and see if it still applies.

Because your paper is really taking shape, you can see what it is going to be like, so you should check it against your outline. If you need to, modify the outline.

51. Remember, each point should be a partial answer to your thesis question.

Refer back to your thesis question and be sure that everything you are writing is still connected to the point you are committed to make.

52. Use quotations only when they say it better than you can.

You want to be sure that this report is mostly yours, so use the writing of other people carefully. This will make your paper stronger. You should have recorded some powerful quotations, so be sure to use them especially if they give your paper added emotional word power or a sense of expertise.

53. Read your paragraphs aloud, and make corrections as needed.

Sometimes students find this embarrassing, even if they are alone, but this is one of the best ways to make sure your paper is good. If you stumble over parts, you should write them or punctuate them so you do not stumble. Most students will probably skip this advice and their papers will suffer.

54. Be sure your paragraphs are connected to each other.

Write a sentence or two at the end of each paragraph to tie it to the next; or write a sentence at the beginning of a paragraph to tie it to the preceding paragraph. These are called transitional sentences, and they bring the reader from one idea to the next. Remember, you want the reader to go through the report easily, and the transition sentences will help. You might have to shift your paragraphs around to make the transitions easier. That is fine.

Your teacher will spend more time on transitional sentences, but let us give you a couple of examples. At the beginning of Chapter IV, we wrote, "By now you have gathered most if not all of your information, and you have to get it into some kind of manageable form, some way to present it in an organized, understandable way that will make the point you wish to make." This sentence refers *back* ("By now you have gathered ...") to the previous chapters, and it looks *ahead* ("... you have to get it into ...") to the work you have to do.

While the preceding example shows a transitional sentence at the beginning of a paragraph, a transitional sentence can also come at the end. When a transitional sentence comes at the end of a paragraph, it goes something like this: "Transitional sentences come in the beginning or the end of a paragraph, but there is one kind of a paragraph that will never have a transitional sentence at the beginning: that is the introductory paragraph, which we will look at in number 55."

55. Write an introductory paragraph.

By now you have pretty much written the body of your report by developing your controlling sentences. Now you will bring it all together by introducing the subject to your reader. This paragraph is a way to introduce the subject, to get the reader interested. You will include some version of the thesis sentence in the paragraph. This lets the reader know what the report is about. You also should give some idea of what major points you are going to cover. This gets tricky, and you will have to write a couple of papers before you really get the hang of it.

It is true that some gifted writers can start with their introductory paragraph and write straight through to the end. While many beginning writers think they can do this, experience shows they cannot, especially if they want to present a good paper for a good grade.

56. Write a concluding paragraph.

This paragraph should be a review of the paper, a restatement of the thesis statement, a confident reminder to the reader that you have done what you said you were going to do. Try to add a sense of power to this, a feeling that you have made your point well.

57. Copy all your work into one continuous paper.

Your paper is about done. You should have a lot of good information that you got from books and that you organized into four or five ideas. You then connected the four or five ideas by means of a thesis question, which you answered and turned around into a thesis statement, supported with your research and writing. You connected your ideas with transitional sentences, and you introduced your reader to your subject. Now, put it all together by writing or typing it into a continuous whole.

Start with your introductory paragraph, then move to your main points, then your conclusion. This is your first rough draft. Professional writers will work on this over and over, but you will probably be satisfied with it in this almost final form.

58. Mark parts that need to be footnoted.

Go back through and make sure that you give credit to any ideas or words that you have taken directly from something you have read, heard, or seen. Our next chapter will tell you how to properly handle these.

59. Edit your writing.

This is a hard part because you want to believe that your paper is finished. You are almost there, but it still needs a little more work. Once again, read it carefully with a pencil in your hand, correcting all spelling and grammatical errors. This is very hard to do since you have been so close to the writing. Often you read what you *wanted* to write instead of what you actually *did write*.

If you have the time, it is best to walk away from the paper for a while. Take a rest. Most accomplished writers put hours or days between the writing and the editing so they can get a fresh approach and see it "new." This time distance gives you a better chance to look at your work more objectively.

If you have a trusted friend or relative, ask that person to read your rough draft over so you can rewrite intelligently. It would be great if you could turn in an error-free report. As you gain experience writing, you will be expected to turn in perfect papers. If you are fortunate enough to have a word processor, you will find editing much easier.

60. Go back over your notes and your first writing and be sure you have not left anything out.

This is the final check to be sure that you said everything you wanted to say.

VI
Report and Term Paper Format

The purpose of this chapter is to show you an example of the points we will discuss on the physical appearance of reports and term papers. As you read the chapter, notice how the various elements of the report are arranged on each page. When you are ready to type your own report, you may use this chapter as a quick guide to the proper format.

John Doe

Research Writing 101

June 1, 1988

VI

Report and Term Paper Format

    A research paper is a formal presentation of your ideas. Since those ideas are supported by information you have found in other people's works, you must give credit to those people through your bibliography and your notes (either footnotes or endnotes). The paper, the bibliography, and the notes should follow an accepted format. The more formal the paper, the more important the format becomes. This chapter will both describe and serve as a model format.

    Your teacher or school may publish a guide that states what your paper should look like. Frequently the history or the English department distributes such a guide. If they do, that is the guide you should follow. If they do not, there are other acceptable guidelines that are very common. One of the most highly respected guides is the <u>MLA Handbook for Writers of Research Papers</u>. In this chapter we have tried to summarize the suggestions found in that book. Another helpful book is the <u>Student's Guide for Writing College Papers</u>, by K. L. Turabian.

It is impossible to type a long paper without making at least a few mistakes. Word processing programs have now made correcting these errors easy and relatively painless. Many word processors also have built-in spelling checkers. A quality paper is not simply one that looks neat and has no spelling errors, it must also have content. But a paper with good content can be hurt by sloppy format and many mechanical errors.

A word processor also allows you to type in the text first and format the paper later. If you must write your paper by hand or type it on a typewriter, you must format the paper <u>while</u> you are typing. Except for page numbers, you should have **one-inch margins** at the top and bottom, and on both sides of the text. **Double-space** your text throughout, including the title of your paper, quotations, notes, and the bibliography; if you are writing the paper by hand, write on every other line, in ink. **Indent five spaces** at the beginning of each new paragraph. And, unlike many books (including this one), your paper should be written, typed, or printed on **only one side**.

It is not necessary to have a **title page**. It is more common to put the title on the first page of the text. If you choose to have a title page, center the title about a third of the page down from the top. Your name, your instructor's name (optional), the course name or number, and the date should appear about two-thirds of the page down from the top and near the right margin. These items should be listed under each other and double-spaced.

It is more common to include the **title** on the first page of the text. In such a format, you should begin one inch from the top of the page and type on separate lines your name, the name of your instructor (optional), the course name or number, and the date. These three or four lines should be double-spaced and flush against the left margin. Then there should be a double space between the date and the title of your paper. Center the title. If the title contains two lines of text, center both lines and double-space between them. Double-space twice more, indent five spaces, and begin typing the first sentence of your paper. Do not underline the title of your paper or put it in quotation marks.

Number all pages consecutively throughout the paper. If you have included a separate title page, do not number it but instead number the first page of text with the number 2. The number should appear in the top right-hand corner, one-half inch from the top. This is the only exception to the one-inch-margin rule.

Quotations are a common feature of research papers. "Quote only words, phrases, lines and passages that are particularly interesting, vivid, unique, or apt, and keep all quotations as brief as possible."[1] Use quotes only when they say things better than you can or when they give your paper added emotional power or a sense of expertise. If the quotation is longer than four typed lines, set it off by beginning a new line and indenting ten spaces from the left margin. The long quote is double-spaced, the same as your text.

Underline all book titles and the names of magazines (periodicals) that appear in the text of your paper. Put **in quotations** the titles of articles from magazines and the titles of chapters from books. A good description of what it was like for displaced families of the 1930s to travel on Highway 66 can be found in an article titled "Route 66: Ghost Road of the Okies" from the August 1977 issue of American Heritage, a magazine we recommend to any student looking for social history.[2] You will notice that in the sentence above, the title of the article was put in quotation marks and the name of the magazine was underlined.

The nature of a research paper requires that you support your ideas and conclusions with information, facts, and other people's statements taken from respected sources. You must, however, acknowledge the sources you used. This is done in the **notes** and **bibliography**. A note is used to tell the reader that what you have just written comes from somewhere else. "It records the origin of, or the authority for, a statement in the text."[3] It gives the reader confidence in what was said and declares that the writer is intellectually honest and acknowledges his or her debt.

If the notes are put at the bottom of the page of text where the citation appears, they are called **footnotes**. Most modern term paper guides suggest **endnotes** instead. Endnotes make typing the paper much easier and serve the same purpose. Endnotes are listed after the text on a new page, which is numbered in the same sequence as the preceding pages.

Center the word "Notes" one inch from the top. Double-space, indent five spaces, and type the **note number** (without punctuation). The note number is typed slightly above the line in both the text and the endnote page. Leave one space and type the endnote reference.[4]

A note has four main parts with a period only at the end: the author's name in normal order followed by a comma, the title, the publishing information in parentheses, and the page number followed by a period. When a note refers to a magazine or newspaper article, you will notice that the date of the magazine or newspaper is in inverted order, for example, June 9, 1942 is written 9 June 1942.

The full note information is given only once. Subsequent notes taken from the same work are given a short form, usually just the author's name and the page number. If you've used two books by the same author, use enough of the title to identify it.

Examples of Footnote or Endnote Format:

Book by one author

¹ Keith Ferrell, <u>John Steinbeck: The Voice of the Land</u> (New York: M. Evans, 1986) 132.

Book by two authors

² Brooks Van Wyck and Otto L. Bettmann, <u>Our Literary Heritage</u> (New York: Dutton, 1956) 237.

Book by an editor

³ Warren G. French, ed., <u>A Companion to</u> The Grapes of Wrath (New York: Viking, 1963) 170.

Book by title (no author listed)

⁴ <u>This Fabulous Century, 1930-1940</u>, vol. 4 of <u>This Fabulous Century</u> (Alexandria: Time-Life, 1969) 134.

Article in a reference book

⁵ Warren G. French, "Steinbeck, John," <u>Encyclopedia Americana</u>, 1981 ed.

Periodical article by author

⁶ D. Aaron, "Radical Humanism of John Steinbeck: <u>The Grapes of Wrath</u> Thirty Years Later," <u>Saturday Review</u> 28 Sept. 1986: 26.

Periodical article by title (no author listed)

⁷ "John Steinbeck, Social Novelist," <u>America</u>   11 Jan. 1969: 32.

The **bibliography** is a list of all materials you have used, even if you did not take anything directly from them. You must, of course, use your judgment; you should not list books you just glanced at and rejected as not helpful. You should list all books and articles you have found useful, even if you used them only for background. The bibliography will list books, magazines, journals, and newspaper articles, and any other sources from which you got information.

Books are the most common entries in bibliographies. The **bibliographic format for books** has three parts: the author, the title, and the publication information. Each part ends with a period and is followed by two spaces. When additional information (such as the edition, or editor's name) is included, a period and two spaces follow each of the items. In listing books, the information is arranged in the following order:

   1. Author's name
   2. Title of the book
   3. Edition, if important
   4. Number of volumes

5. Place of publication, name of publisher, and date of publication

Examples of Books in a Bibliography:

Book by one author

Ferrell, Keith. <u>John Steinbeck: The Voice of the Land</u>. New York: M. Evans, 1986.

Book by two authors

Van Wyck, Brooks, and Otto L. Bettmann. <u>Our Literary Heritage</u>. New York: Dutton, 1956.

Book by an editor

French, Warren, ed. <u>A Companion to</u> The Grapes of Wrath. New York: Viking, 1963.

Book by title (no author listed)

<u>This Fabulous Century, 1930-1940</u>. Vol. 4 of <u>This Fabulous Century</u>. Alexandria: Time-Life, 1969.

Article in a reference book

French, Warren G. "Steinbeck, John." <u>Encyclopedia Americana</u>. 1981 ed.

The **bibliographic format for periodicals** (magazines, journals, pamphlets) is similar to that for books. The entry for an article has three main parts: the author, the title of the article, and the publication information. The only unfamiliar part may be the volume number. Many magazines and journals include a volume number as well as a date to distinguish each issue. In listing periodicals, the information is arranged in the following order:

1. Author's name
2. Title of the article
3. Name of the periodical
4. Volume number, if it has one
5. Date of publication
6. Page numbers of the entire article

Examples of Periodicals in a Bibliography:

Periodical article by author

Aaron, D. "Radical Humanism of John Steinbeck: The Grapes of
    Wrath Thirty Years Later." Saturday Review 28 Sept. 1968:
    14.

Periodical article by title (no author listed)

"John Steinbeck, Social Novelist." America 11 Jan. 1969: 512-
    28.

The **notes** are listed on a separate page immediately following the text. They are numbered sequentially to correspond with the numbers used within the text. The **bibliography** is also begun on a new page, immediately following the notes. The entries are alphabetized by author. If there is no author, they are alphabetized using the first word of the title. The words <u>the</u>, <u>a</u>, and <u>an</u> are ignored if they begin the title.

Chapter 6 Notes

[1] Joseph Gibaldi and Walter S. Achtert, <u>MLA Handbook for Writers of Research Papers</u>, 2nd ed. (New York: MLA, 1984) 48.

[2] Thomas W. Pew, "Route 66: Ghost Road of the Okies," <u>American Heritage</u> Aug. 1977: 24.

[3] Jacques Barzun and Henry F. Graff, <u>The Modern Researcher</u>, 4th ed. (San Diego: Harcourt Brace Jovanovich, 1985) 359.

[4] Gibaldi and Achtert 167.

Chapter 6 Bibliography

Barzun, Jacques, and Henry F. Graff. <u>The Modern Researcher</u>. 4th ed. New York: Harcourt Brace Jovanovich, 1985.

<u>The Chicago Manual of Style</u>. 13th ed. Chicago: University of Chicago Press, 1982.

Garcia-Barrio, Constance. "Putting It in Writing: Preparing Reports That Put You at the Top of Your Class or Career." <u>Essence Magazine</u>. Nov. 1984: 37.

Gibaldi, Joseph, and Walter S. Achtert. <u>MLA Handbook for Writers of Research Papers</u>. 2nd ed. New York: Modern Language Association, 1984.

Strunk, William, and E. B. White. <u>The Elements of Style</u>. New York: Macmillan, 1959.

Turabian, Kate L. <u>Student's Guide for Writing College Papers</u>. 3rd ed. Chicago: University of Chicago Press, 1976.

www.ingramcontent.com/pod-product-compliance
Lightning Source LLC
Chambersburg PA
CBHW070650300426
44111CB00013B/2359